HOW TO DRAW
SHIPS

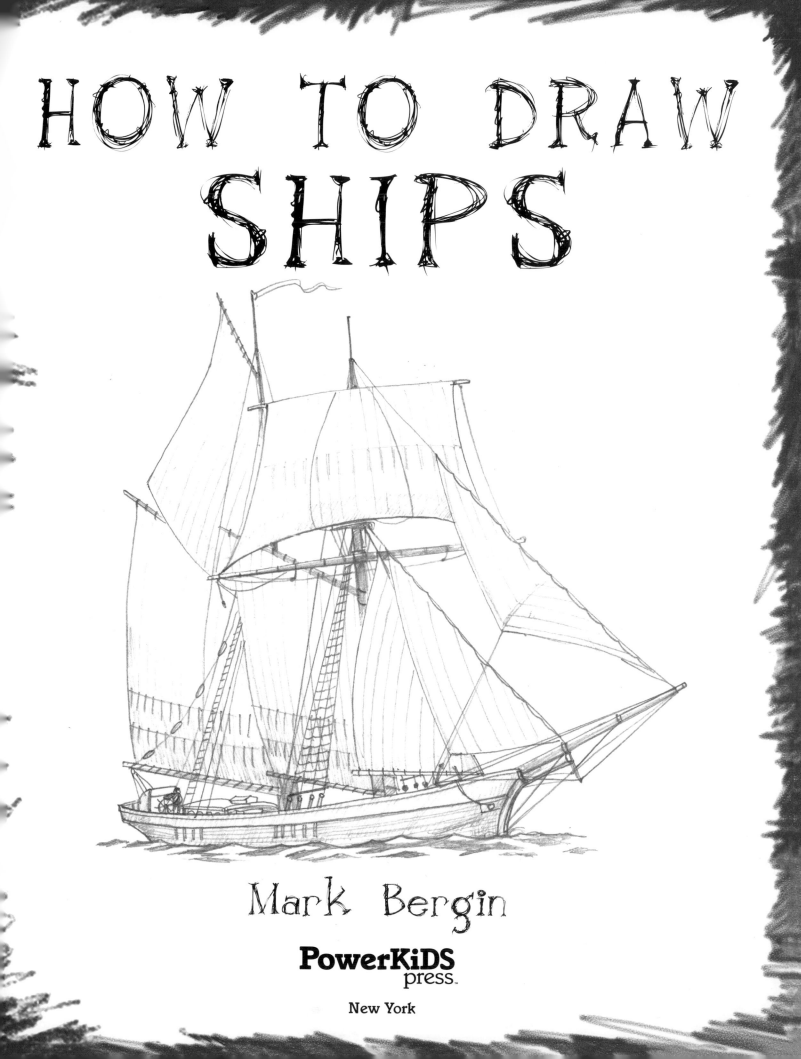

Mark Bergin

PowerKiDS
press

New York

Published in 2011 by The Rosen Publishing Group, Inc.
29 East 21st Street, New York, NY 10010

Editor: Rob Walker
U.S. Editor: Kara Murray

Library of Congress Cataloging-in-Publication Data

Bergin, Mark.
  How to draw ships / Mark Bergin. —1st ed.
      p. cm.
  Includes index.
  ISBN 978-1-4488-1577-7 (library binding) — ISBN 978-1-4488-1599-9 (pbk.) —
ISBN 978-1-4488-1600-2 (6-pack)
  1. Ships in art—Juvenile literature. 2. Drawing—Technique—Juvenile literature. I. Title.
  NC825.S5B47 2011
  743'.837—dc22
                              2010011573

Manufactured in Heshan, China

CPSIA Compliance Information: Batch #SS0102PK: For Further Information contact Rosen Publishing, New York, New York at 1-800-237-9932

Contents

Making a Start

Learning to draw is about looking and seeing. Keep practicing, and get to know your subject. Use a sketchbook to make quick sketches. Start by doodling, and experiment with shapes and patterns. There are many ways to draw. This book shows some of them. Visit art galleries, look at artists' drawings, see how friends draw, but above all, find your own way.

Pencil

Large felt-tip pen

Remember that practice makes
perfect. If it looks wrong, start again.
Keep working at it. The more you
draw, the more you will learn.

Ballpoint pen

Fineliner pen

Felt-tip pen

Perspective

If you look at any object from different viewpoints, you will see that the part that is closest to you looks larger and the part farthest away from you looks smaller. Drawing in perspective is a way of creating a feeling of depth—of showing three dimensions on a flat surface.

It may help you with perspective if you imagine your object fitted into a rectangular block like this.

V.P.

The vanishing point (V.P.) is the place in a perspective drawing where parallel lines appear to meet. The position of the vanishing point depends on the viewer's eye level. Sometimes a low viewpoint can give your drawing added drama.

Two-point perspective uses two vanishing points: one for lines running along the length of the object, and one on the opposite side for lines running across the width of the object.

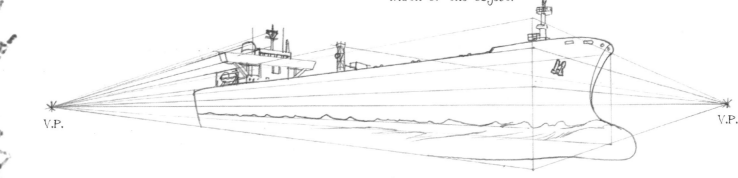

V.P.   V.P.

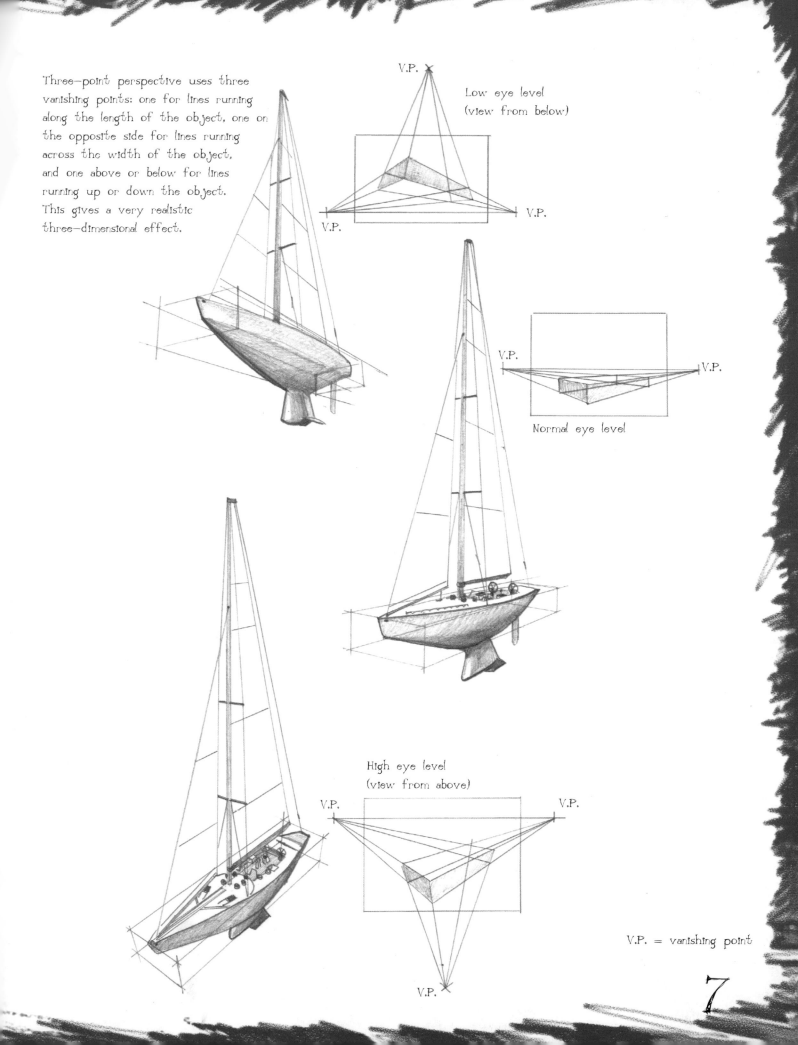

Three-point perspective uses three vanishing points: one for lines running along the length of the object, one on the opposite side for lines running across the width of the object, and one above or below for lines running up or down the object. This gives a very realistic three-dimensional effect.

V.P.

Low eye level
(view from below)

V.P.

V.P.

V.P.

Normal eye level

High eye level
(view from above)

V.P.

V.P.

V.P.

V.P. = vanishing point

7

Photographs

Drawing from photographs can help you practice your drawing skills. It is important that you consider the position of your drawing on the paper. This is called composition.

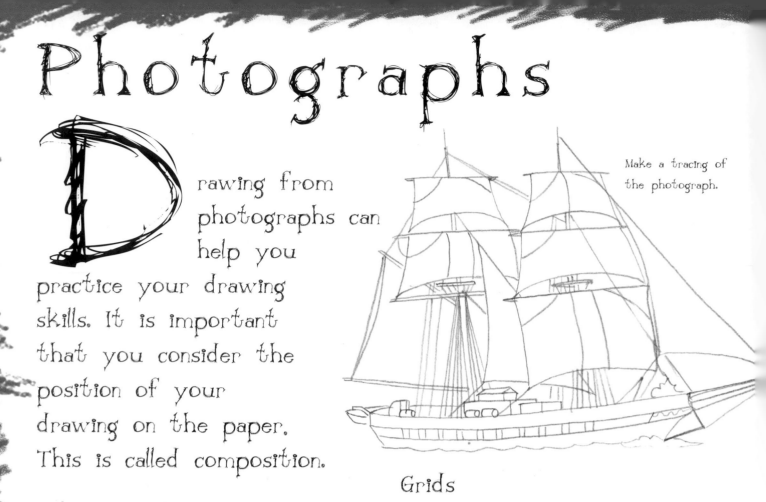

Make a tracing of the photograph.

Grids

Using a grid to help you enlarge a drawing is called squaring up.

Lightly draw a grid over your traced image.

Light source

Decide which direction the light is coming from in your drawing. Add shadows on the parts of the ship that face away from the light.

Lightly draw a grid on your drawing paper, using larger squares than before but keeping the same proportions. You can now copy the shapes in each square of your tracing onto your drawing paper.

Add more tone and detail to finish the drawing.

Add a background to give atmosphere to your drawing.

9

Drawing Sails

Sails are large pieces of fabric used to catch the wind to propel a boat or ship. The shape of a sail changes depending on how the wind catches it.

Here you can see how the shape of a sail changes depending on the direction of the wind.

Wind direction

Wind direction

Wind direction

There are many different types of sailing craft. There is huge variation in the shape, the number of sails, and the formation they take.

Bermuda rig

Sloop

Spritsail barge

Yawl or ketch

Schooner

Brigantine

Brig

Topsail schooner

Square-rigged ship

Large racing yachts

Sketching

Y ou can't always rely on your memory, so you have to look around and find real–life things you want to draw. Using a sketchbook is one of the best ways to build up drawing skills. Learn to observe objects: see how they move, how they are made, and how they work. What you draw should be what you have seen. Since the fifteenth century, artists have used sketchbooks to record their ideas.

Sketching models

Try drawing model ships and boats. You can look closely and start to understand your subject.

A harbor is a good place to start. There are many different types of boats that you can draw in an interesting setting.

Sketching

A quick sketch can often capture as much information as a careful drawing that has taken many hours.

Speedboat

Speedboats are designed to move quickly through the water. They are propelled by powerful motors at the stern.

First draw a three-dimensional rectangular box. Then draw a line through the center.

Using the center line as a starting point, draw long, curved lines to show the shape of the boat.

The stern (rear) of the boat is drawn with straight lines.

Draw straight lines on the bottom of the rectangular box to mark the bottom of the boat.

14

Start to draw the top of the boat. Using straight lines, add the windows.

Sketch the checkerboard design running down the side of the boat.

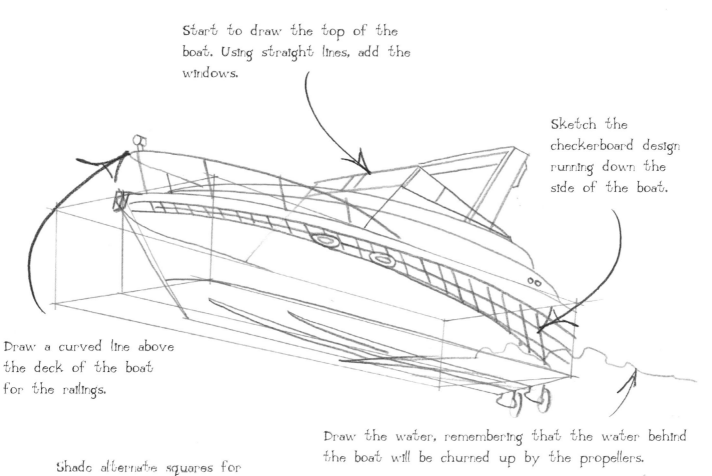

Draw a curved line above the deck of the boat for the railings.

Shade alternate squares for the checkerboard design.

Draw the water, remembering that the water behind the boat will be churned up by the propellers.

Add details such as people and an antenna.

Using a Mirror
You can often see mistakes in a drawing by looking at it in reverse in a mirror.

Shade the water underneath and also the boat's underside.

Add more detail to the water.

Finish by removing any unwanted construction lines.

Racing Yacht

Yacht races are held all around the world. The yachts used are specially designed to take full advantage of the wind and move very fast through the water.

Mast

Draw two long lines for the mast.

Start by drawing a narrow rectangle for the hull.

Draw a straight line for the water.

Add a line to form a small triangle to make the stern of the boat.

Draw a straight line down from the mast to the bow (front) of the boat.

Add a straight line coming down from the top of the mast to the stern of the boat.

Add curves to the bow of the boat.

Add the keel.

Add a small rudder.

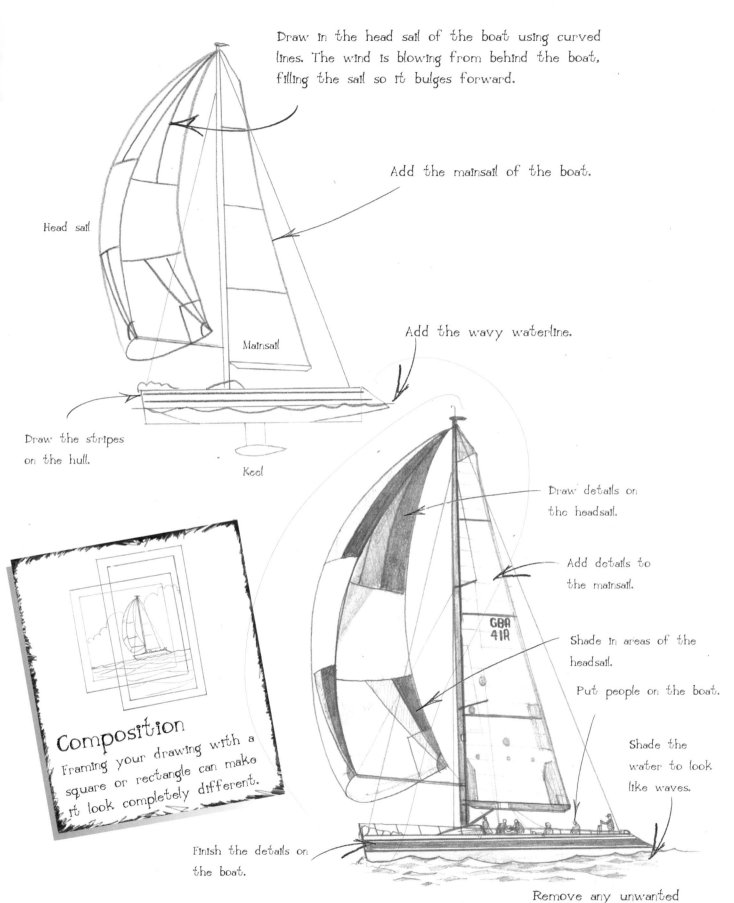

Draw in the head sail of the boat using curved lines. The wind is blowing from behind the boat, filling the sail so it bulges forward.

Add the mainsail of the boat.

Head sail

Mainsail

Add the wavy waterline.

Draw the stripes on the hull.

Keel

Draw details on the headsail.

Add details to the mainsail.

GBA 41A

Shade in areas of the headsail.

Put people on the boat.

Shade the water to look like waves.

Composition
Framing your drawing with a square or rectangle can make it look completely different.

Finish the details on the boat.

Remove any unwanted construction lines.

Rowboat

This traditional rowboat is a small craft made out of wood. It needs oars to propel it through the water.

First draw a three-dimensional box with a center line through its middle.

Inside this box, draw curved lines to form the shape of the boat. The stern should be the same height as the box, but the bow rises above it.

The keel on a rowing boat runs its entire length. Add it in with curved lines.

Draw a long, curved line for the bottom of the boat.

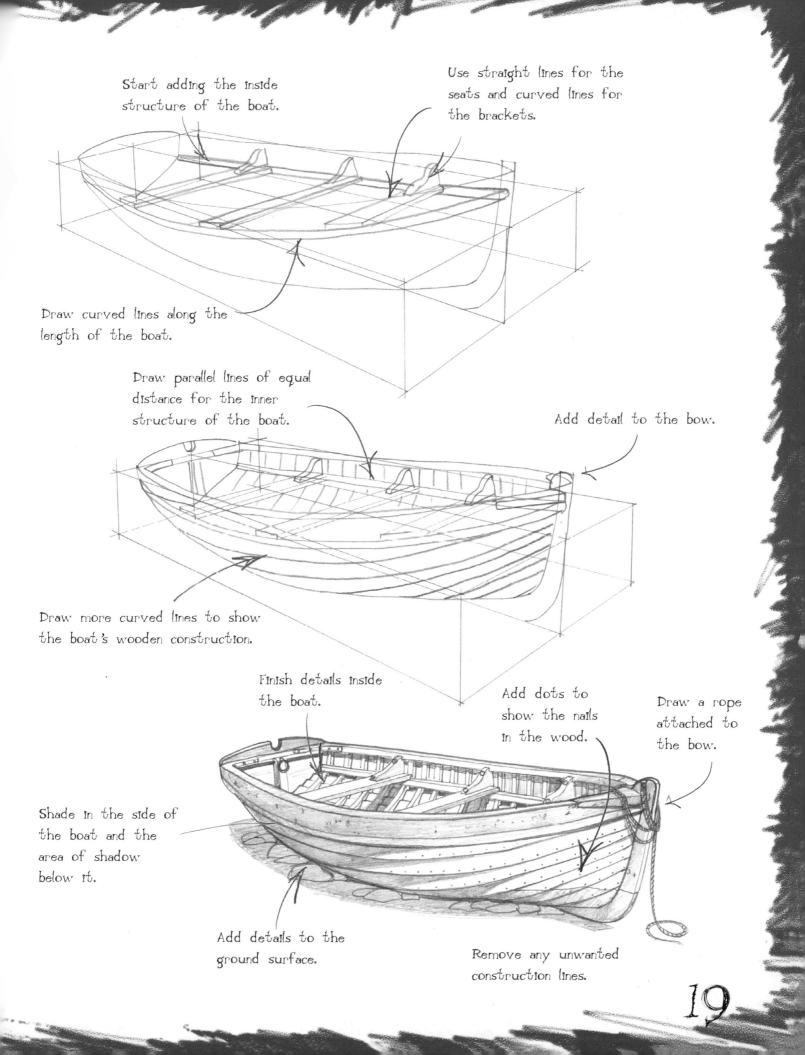

Start adding the inside structure of the boat.

Use straight lines for the seats and curved lines for the brackets.

Draw curved lines along the length of the boat.

Draw parallel lines of equal distance for the inner structure of the boat.

Add detail to the bow.

Draw more curved lines to show the boat's wooden construction.

Finish details inside the boat.

Add dots to show the nails in the wood.

Draw a rope attached to the bow.

Shade in the side of the boat and the area of shadow below it.

Add details to the ground surface.

Remove any unwanted construction lines.

Topsail Schooner

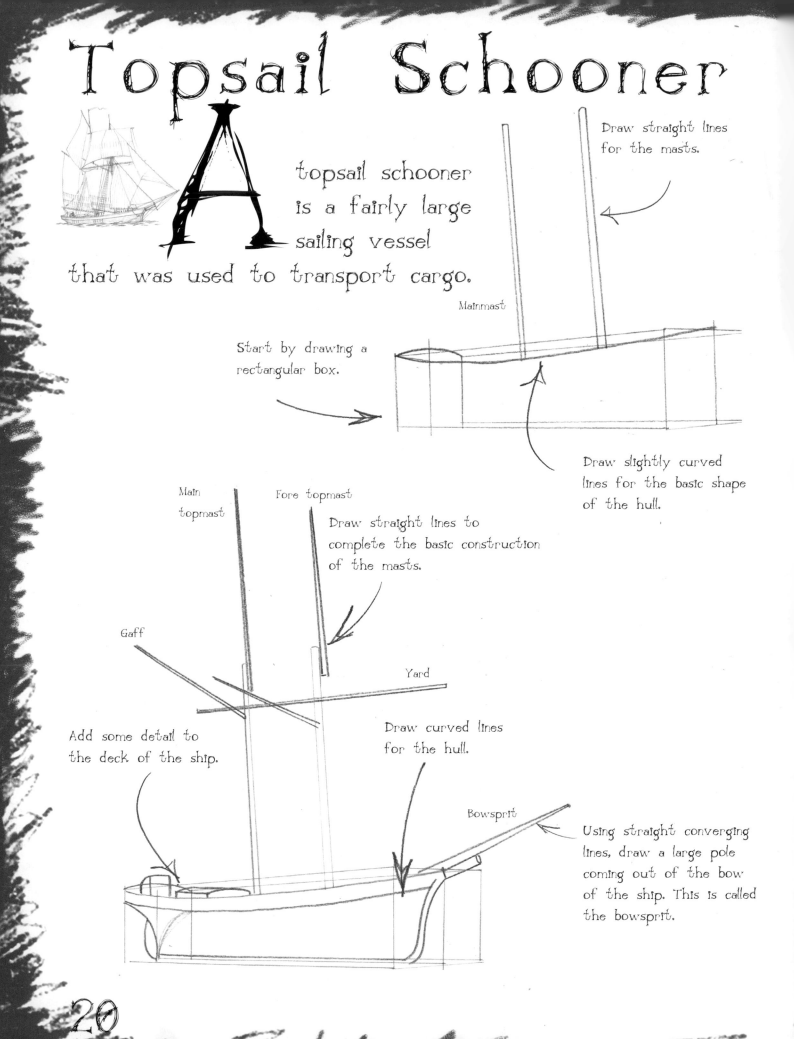

A topsail schooner is a fairly large sailing vessel that was used to transport cargo.

Draw straight lines for the masts.

Mainmast

Start by drawing a rectangular box.

Draw slightly curved lines for the basic shape of the hull.

Main topmast

Fore topmast

Draw straight lines to complete the basic construction of the masts.

Gaff

Yard

Add some detail to the deck of the ship.

Draw curved lines for the hull.

Bowsprit

Using straight converging lines, draw a large pole coming out of the bow of the ship. This is called the bowsprit.

Draw in the basic shape of each sail.

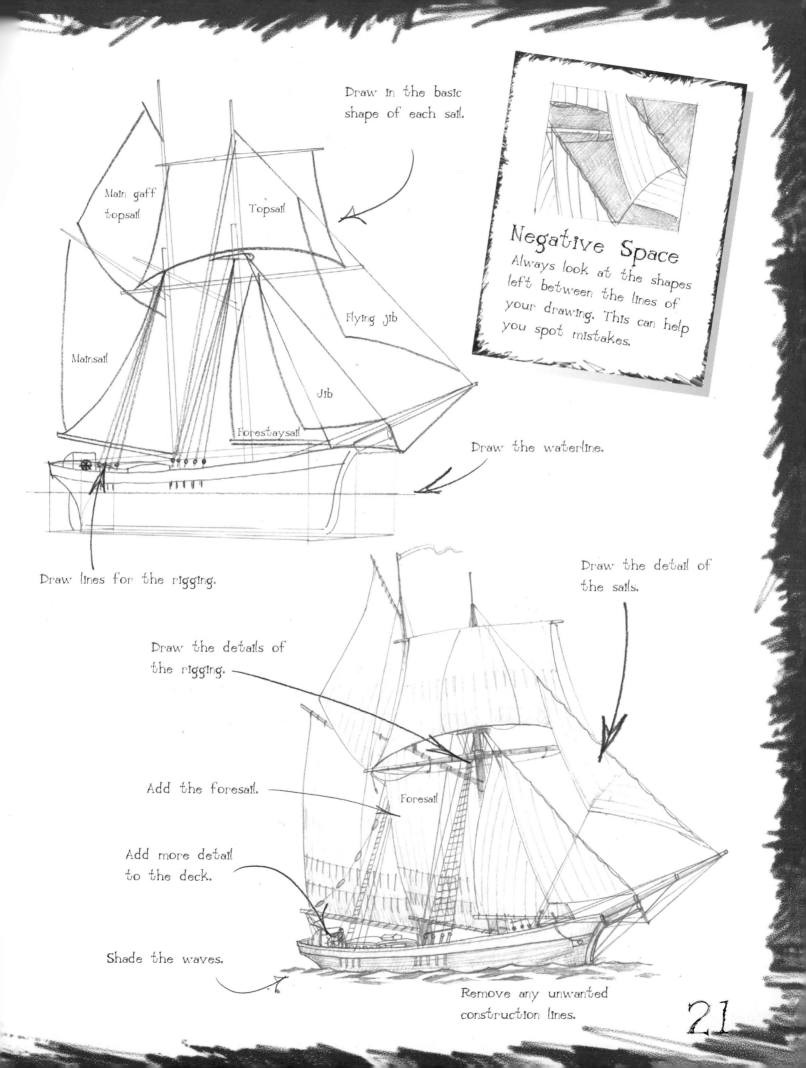

Main gaff topsail

Topsail

Flying Jib

Mainsail

Jib

Forestaysail

Draw the waterline.

Draw lines for the rigging.

Negative Space

Always look at the shapes left between the lines of your drawing. This can help you spot mistakes.

Draw the details of the rigging.

Add the foresail.

Foresail

Add more detail to the deck.

Shade the waves.

Draw the detail of the sails.

Remove any unwanted construction lines.

21

Ocean Tanker

An ocean tanker is a massive ship used to transport huge amounts of fuel.

Ships and Water
To make your drawing look authentic, the ship should always be sitting in the water, not on top of it.

Start your drawing with a large rectangular box with a center line through the middle.

Using the lines of your original rectangular box as a guide, draw box shapes on the ship's deck where the superstructure will be.

Draw a curved lip to indicate the top of the bow.

Draw curved lines to mark the shape of the ship's bow.

22

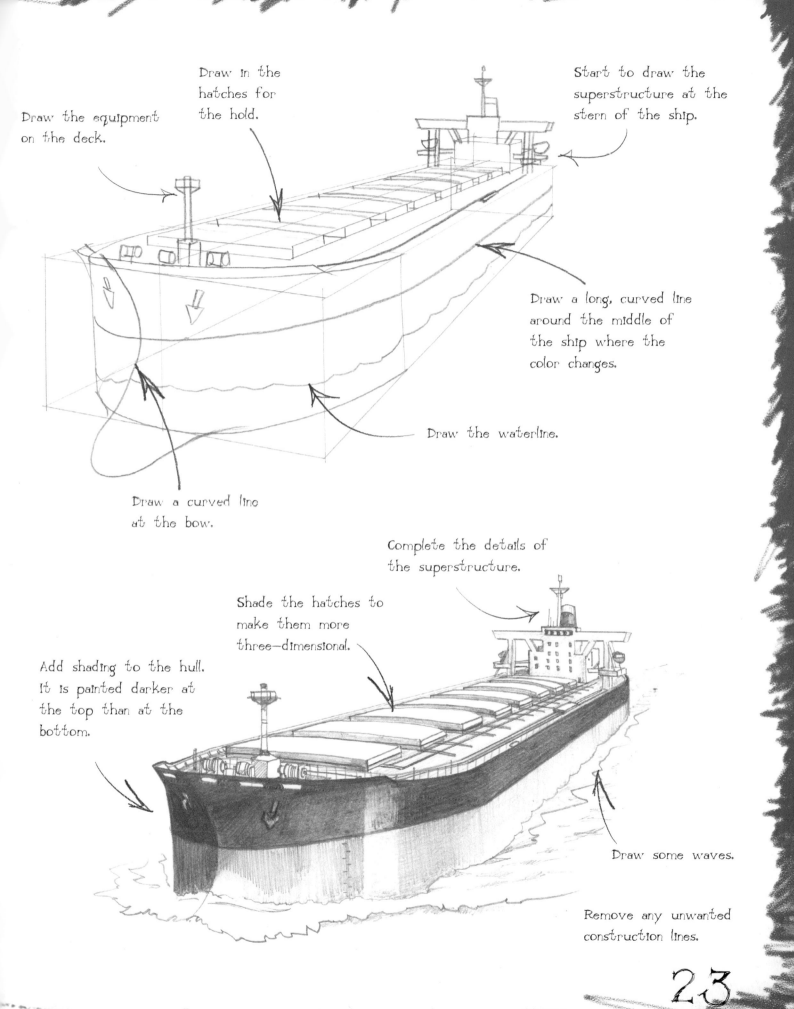

Draw the equipment
on the deck.

Draw in the
hatches for
the hold.

Start to draw the
superstructure at the
stern of the ship.

Draw a long, curved line
around the middle of
the ship where the
color changes.

Draw the waterline.

Draw a curved line
at the bow.

Complete the details of
the superstructure.

Shade the hatches to
make them more
three-dimensional.

Add shading to the hull.
It is painted darker at
the top than at the
bottom.

Draw some waves.

Remove any unwanted
construction lines.

23

Fishing Boat

T his small fishing boat is a working vessel that travels out to sea to try to catch a good haul of fish.

Start your drawing with a three-dimensional rectangular box with a center line through the middle.

Begin the main hull of the boat by drawing curved lines. The stern is the same height as the box, but the bow rises above it.

Add a curved line for the stern of the boat.

The keel for this boat curves down the bow but straightens along the bottom of the hull.

24

Add a small houselike structure at the bow.

Add the main bridge structure to the deck.

Add more curved lines to the side of the boat.

Draw straight lines for the ropes of the fishing equipment.

Use straight lines to draw the arms of the fishing equipment.

Draw the winch machinery.

Add detail to the bridge.

Darken the underside of the lines on the side of the boat to give a realistic shadow effect.

Add the water surface.

Remove any unwanted construction lines.

25

Ocean Liner

This luxury ocean liner is a large sea—going vessel designed to transport many people in great comfort.

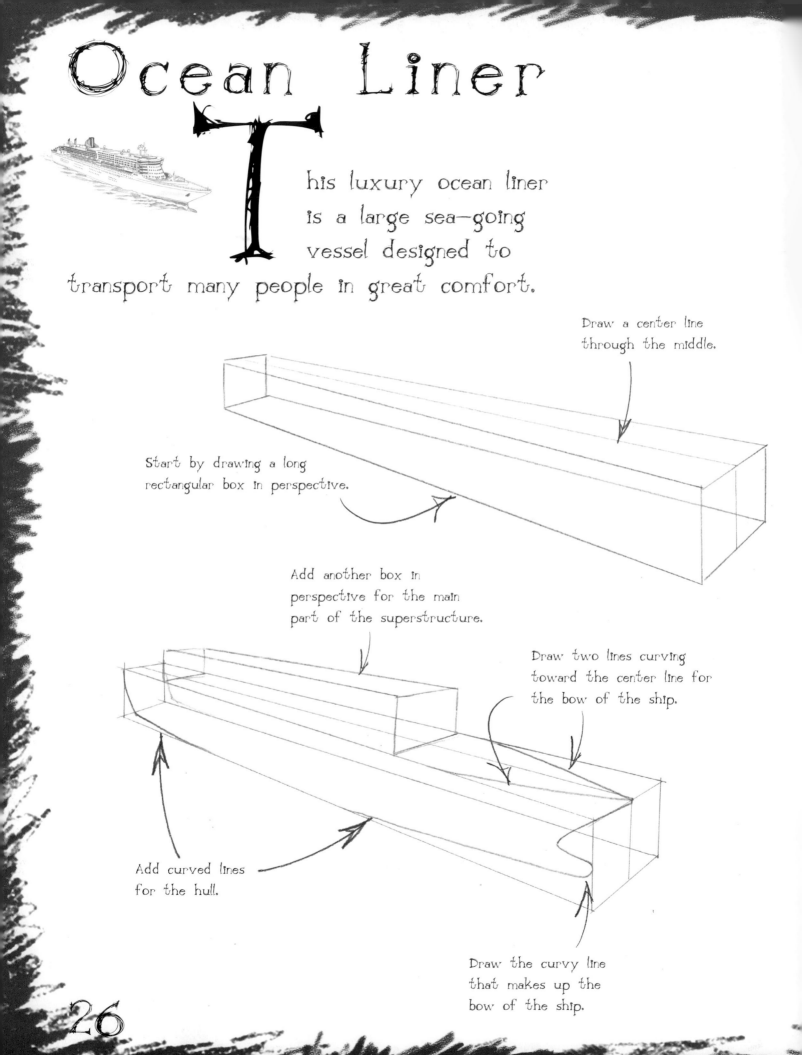

Draw a center line through the middle.

Start by drawing a long rectangular box in perspective.

Add another box in perspective for the main part of the superstructure.

Draw two lines curving toward the center line for the bow of the ship.

Add curved lines for the hull.

Draw the curvy line that makes up the bow of the ship.

Add the funnels.

Add detail to the front of the main superstructure.

Draw the waterline.

Add guidelines along the upper decks to help you position the windows.

Sketch a line for the window of the bridge.

Add small shapes for the lifeboats.

Using the straight lines as a guide, finish the detail of the windows.

Complete the details of the superstructure.

Add tone to the drawing to give it more impact.

Add small dots for the portholes.

Add small areas of shading to represent the waves.

Remove any unwanted construction lines.

27

Lifeboat

Lifeboats play a crucial role along coastal areas. These boats need to be fast, steady, and durable to carry out rescues in difficult conditions.

First draw a perspective box with a center line down the middle.

Add another three-dimensional box for the cabin on the deck.

Use straight lines for the front section of the cabin.

Add a curved line to create the bow.

Draw a straight line for the front of the bow.

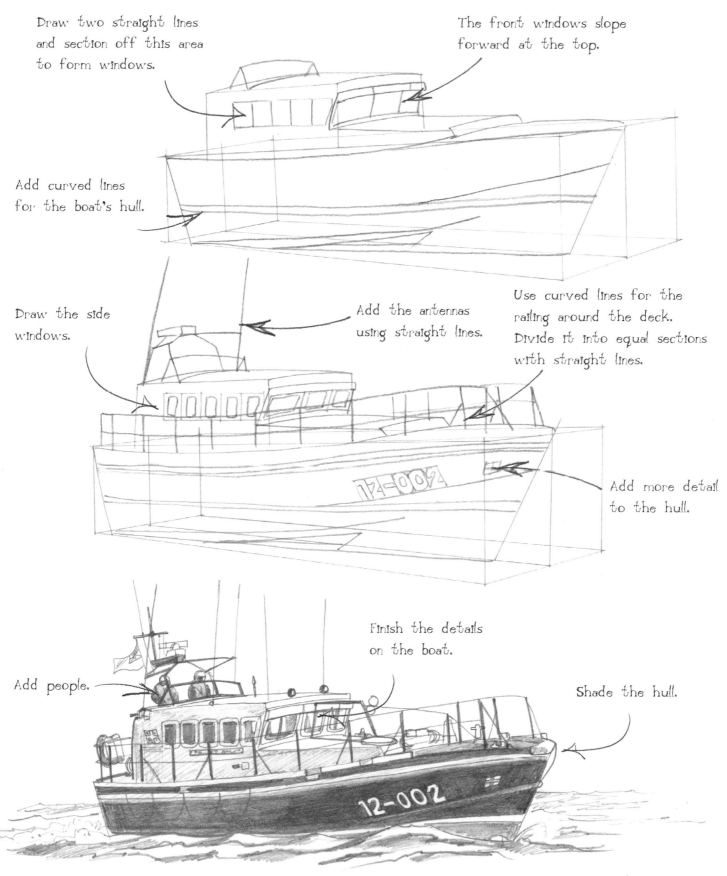

Draw two straight lines and section off this area to form windows.

The front windows slope forward at the top.

Add curved lines for the boat's hull.

Draw the side windows.

Add the antennas using straight lines.

Use curved lines for the railing around the deck. Divide it into equal sections with straight lines.

Add more detail to the hull.

174-002

Finish the details on the boat.

Add people.

Shade the hull.

12-002

Add waves with sketchy lines and shading.

Remove any unwanted construction lines.

29

Harbor Scene

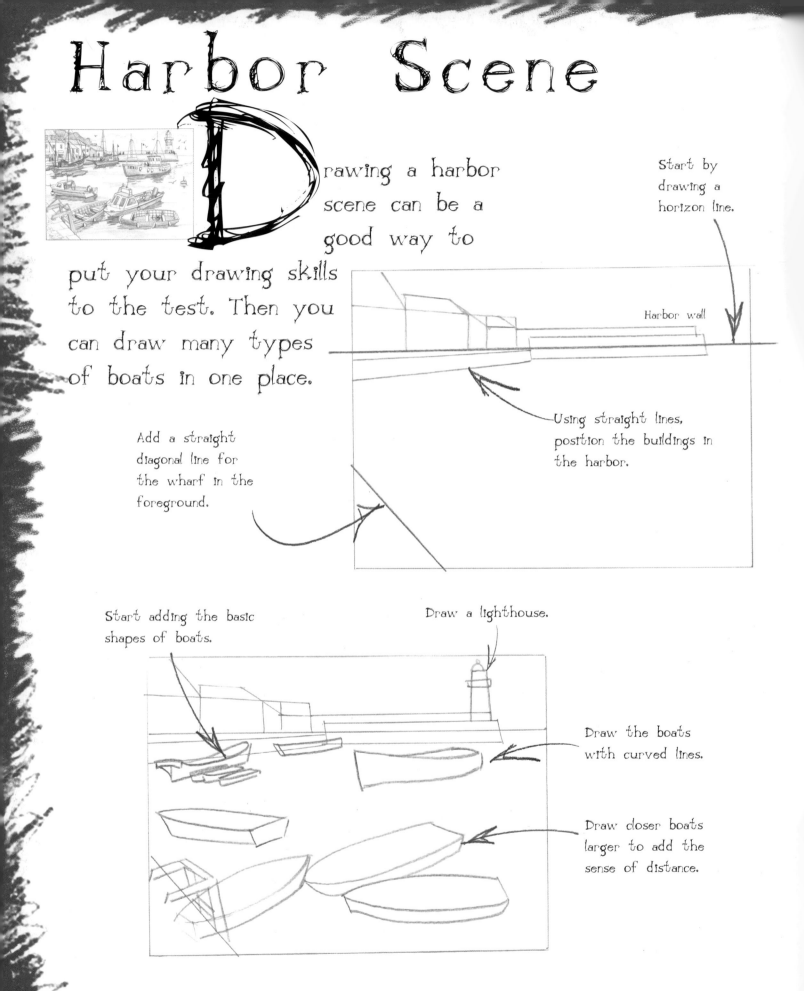

Drawing a harbor scene can be a good way to put your drawing skills to the test. Then you can draw many types of boats in one place.

Start by drawing a horizon line.

Harbor wall

Using straight lines, position the buildings in the harbor.

Add a straight diagonal line for the wharf in the foreground.

Start adding the basic shapes of boats.

Draw a lighthouse.

Draw the boats with curved lines.

Draw closer boats larger to add the sense of distance.

Add detail to the buildings in the harbor.

Add more detail to the boats' shapes.

Draw as many different types of boats as you want.

Draw handrails on the steps going down to the water.

Add clouds and seagulls to the background for atmosphere.

Add reflections of the boats in the water.

Add shading to each of the boats.

Finish the details on the boats.

Remove any unwanted construction lines.

Glossary

bow (BOW) The front of a boat or ship.

composition (kom—puh—ZIH—shun) The positioning of a picture on the drawing paper.

construction lines (kun—STRUK—shun LYNZ) Guidelines used in the early stages of a drawing, usually erased later.

hold (HOHLD) The part of a ship where the cargo is stored.

hull (HUL) The main body of a boat or ship.

keel (KEEL) The ridge that runs along the bottom of the hull.

light source (LYT SAWRS) The direction from which the light seems to come in a drawing.

negative space (NEH—guh—tiv SPAYS) The empty space left between objects or parts of objects.

rudder (RUH—dur) The hinged flap at the stern of a boat that is used to steer it.

stern (STERN) The rear of a boat or ship.

three—dimensional (three—deh—MENCH—nul) Having an effect of depth, so as to look lifelike or real.

yard (YARD) A horizontal pole attached to a mast, from which a sail is hung.

Index

Web Sites

Due to the changing nature of Internet links, PowerKids Press has developed an online list of Web sites related to the subject of this book. This site is updated regularly. Please use this link to access the list:

www.powerkidslinks.com/howtodraw/ships/